Contents

1 Why remember the Boyne?

Many countries have a day when people celebrate some event which they see as specially significant in their history. The Fourth of July commemorates the Declaration of Independence in the USA and, for the French, Bastille Day marks the founding of the French Republic. In Ireland two different events are celebrated. In the Republic, Easter Monday is remembered as heralding the separation of the 26 counties from the United Kingdom. In Northern Ireland, the Twelfth of July is a public holiday to mark the anniversary of the Battle of the Boyne. Why does this battle seem so important, three hundred years after it took place?

A Wall-painting of William of Orange

NO SURRENDER

Two traditions

The wall-painting of William of Orange shows the best-known folk-hero among the Protestants in Northern Ireland. King Billy of popular songs and stories, is the man who beat the Catholic James II at the Battle of the Boyne. 'No surrender' refers to the siege of Londonderry, which is a close second to the battle in Protestant folk history. Together the siege and battle present a story of suffering endured with courage which ends with a triumphal outcome.

The Catholic and nationalist tradition naturally does not celebrate the Battle of the Boyne. Its popular history of that period focuses on the treaty which ended the fighting a year later. This was the Treaty of Limerick, promising Irish Catholics a fair deal. According to the nationalist version this treaty was broken by England and the Protestants as soon as they had the upper hand.

WHY
REMEMBER
THE BOYNE?

QUESTIONS IN

IRISH
history

George Power
General editor: John Robottom

QUESTIONS IN

IRISH
history

The Teaching of History Trust was created in 1986 for the development of a series of books on Irish History. Its Advisory Committee included historians, inspectors and teachers from Northern Ireland, the Republic of Ireland and England.

Until his death in March 1991, the Committee's Chairman was Professor R.H.C. Davis who did so much to ensure the realisation of the series. Advisers and authors alike owe him a dept of gratitude for his vision and commitment. The books are dedicated to him.

These are the traditions but they cannot be traced back to 1689, 1690 or 1691. They were created in later years to build up a picture of the past which suited the views of people in the nineteenth and twentieth centuries. The Protestants of Ulster did not hero-worship King Billy for a hundred years after the Battle of the Boyne. The Orange Society, which later became the Orange Order, was only founded in 1795 and it was actually banned for a time in the 1830s on suspicion of plotting against the British king. The story of the broken Treaty of Limerick was known to Catholic peasants and labourers only from the time of O'Connell's great nationalist campaigns in the 1820s.

What is this book about?

This book tries to explain what really happened. To understand this we need to begin by asking what Ireland and her people were like at the time. Most people were strongly influenced by their religious views but there were other things to concern them. Should they be more obedient to their king or to their local landlord? What was the best way of looking after their own safety and the future of their children? Could they avoid taking sides or would they be forced to become involved? The outcome may seem clear to us but people at that time could not be sure what the next few years would bring.

Then we need to ask how much the events around the Battle of the Boyne and the siege of Limerick were really about Ireland itself. James II was king of Ireland simply because he inherited it, along with England and Scotland, when his elder brother died. In 1688 he was driven from the English throne and fled to France. After that, he saw Ireland as the best stepping-stone on the way to regaining the throne of England.

The new king of England, William of Orange, was a Dutchman and the leader of a great alliance of European countries against France. He had to stop James and the French king, Louis XIV, from using Ireland as a base to attack England and weaken the alliance. In this way one stage in the long struggle between France and her enemies happened to take place in Ireland. Yet, in the end, Ireland's future depended on the fighting on land and sea between European countries.

Why was the Battle of the Boyne important?

Although it was just part of a wider struggle, the battle was still important for the people of Ireland. James II's Irish army and his French allies were defeated and he had to flee the country, leaving the Protestant Irish and English supporters of William in control. This led to what is sometimes called the 'Protestant Ascendancy'. There had been discrimination against Catholics for more than a hundred years but it now became more severe.

In Ulster, the Protestant Ascendancy turned out to mean a return of discrimination against Presbyterians. The centre of the Ascendancy was Dublin where Protestant Irish and Anglo-Irish landlords had their town houses, met in Parliament and controlled every branch of government and the law. Ulster was by no means a centre of loyalism. It was an area to be watched for signs of Presbyterian unrest and disloyalty to the British crown.

Before you study the rest of this book, make a summary of what you have heard or seen about the siege of Londonderry, the Battle of the Boyne, the Treaty of Limerick, James II and William of Orange. Add to it by making a survey among friends and relatives. Keep it to see how much your views have changed after you have completed the study.

2 Before the Boyne: How did the Irish live?

What kind of life did people lead in different parts of Ireland? John Dunton, an English bookseller travelled through the island in the late 1690s. His letters home give us some answers to the question.

Herdsmen in the west

In 1699 John Dunton, arrived at a village in Connemara with his guide and interpreter. They were offered hospitality in the best house. Their hosts cooked a hare which the guide's greyhound had caught on the way. They also gave the travellers oatcakes:

A Hospitality in Connemara

A1 " [and] . . . a greate roll of fresh butter of three pounds at least and a wooden vessel full of milk and water."

After supper they settled down to sleep on a bed of rushes on the floor with two thick wool blankets. A little later they were disturbed by someone opening the door to let in some cows and sheep. John Dunton was afraid that the animals would tread on him, but they kept to their own end of the room. They were brought in every night for fear of wolves.

When John Dunton was leaving the next morning he offered money to his hosts:

A2 ". . . but they refused it with some marks of displeasure because they were of the gentry."

Dunton then visited the head of the most important family in the area, who was known in the Gaelic way as The O'Flaherty. Dunton was surprised to see that the house was just a larger version of the one he had stayed in the night before. It was a single room with a fire in the middle of the earth floor, wattle and mud walls, and a roof thatched with rushes. His guide explained that this was The O'Flaherty's booley, a summer home, used only when the cattle were being grazed on the higher mountains. Dunton joined in a deer hunt with thirty huntsmen and eighteen hounds, and enjoyed a venison feast afterwards.

Farmers in the central plain

Dunton found life more humdrum but more comfortable in the central plain. Here farmers had long ago cleared the trees to make space for livestock and crops. Dunton described the garden plots of the small farmers in Kildare:

B Gardens of the Kildare farmers

"Behind one of their cabins lies the garden, a piece of ground sometimes of half an acre and in this is the turf stack, their corn, perhaps 200 to 300 sheaves of oats and as much peas. The rest of the ground is full of their dearly-beloved potatoes and a few cabbages."

Most farmers also reared a few cattle and sheep to sell to dealers at local fairs. In some homes there were spinning wheels and perhaps a loom, so part of the family income came from spinning and weaving wool or linen. Dunton noted that the farmers had a little money to spend on new luxuries such as tea, sugar and tobacco. Both men and women smoked pipes.

He saw evidence that visiting relatives and neighbours was a part of everyday life, not just an occasional escape from work. Weddings and wakes were important events, with plenty of food and drink, music and dancing. Hurling matches between the young men of different parishes attracted big crowds. The girls and children cheered their teams and:

C A day out at the hurling match

1 *How was life in the central plain different from life in the west in (a) agriculture (b) the use of money (c) social life?*

"... the elder people sit spectators, telling stories of their own like feats in days of yore, and now and then divert themselves with a quill-full of sneezing or a whiff of tobacco."

Inland towns

The inland towns of the 1690s often had only a few hundred inhabitants. Many still had their old walls even though these were crumbling and some houses had been built outside them. The townspeople included craftsmen such as blacksmiths and carpenters, and there were pedlars who took small articles for sale round the villages. There would be a few merchants dealing in timber, hides, wool and butter, and fairs were held for buying and selling. Unless a town was on an important trade route it would not be very prosperous.

D John Dunton describes Kildare

"... but a poor place not lying in any road and not having any trade belonging to it."

Ports

Ireland's largest towns were the ports: Dublin, Cork, Galway, Limerick and Belfast. They all had quays for loading and unloading the ships which brought in luxuries from abroad and sailed away with salted meat, hides, leather and wool. Near the quays were warehouses and busy workshops such as tanyards for making leather, coopers' yards where barrels and casks were made, and sheds where beef and pork were salted.

A merchant in a sea-port was likely to be much wealthier than one in a country town. His large, stone-built house would have his counting-house and warehouse beside it and he employed several clerks, carters and other workpeople.

Dublin

Dublin was the largest town, with a population of over 40,000 which was more than any town in England apart from London. As well as a port it was a centre of crafts and manufactures. Many noblemen had town houses there. Government officials, army officers and judges lived there too. Each year more houses were built on the south side of the Liffey. Dublin had its university, Trinity College, a theatre and coffee houses. The main streets were lit at night and there were hackney carriages for hire.

E Views of Dublin

E1 *A French visitor writes*

" . . . one of the greatest and best peopled towns in Europe, and the residence of all the nobility of the Kingdom of Ireland."

(Jorevin de Rocheford, 1666–1668)

E2 *Dublin in the seventeenth century*

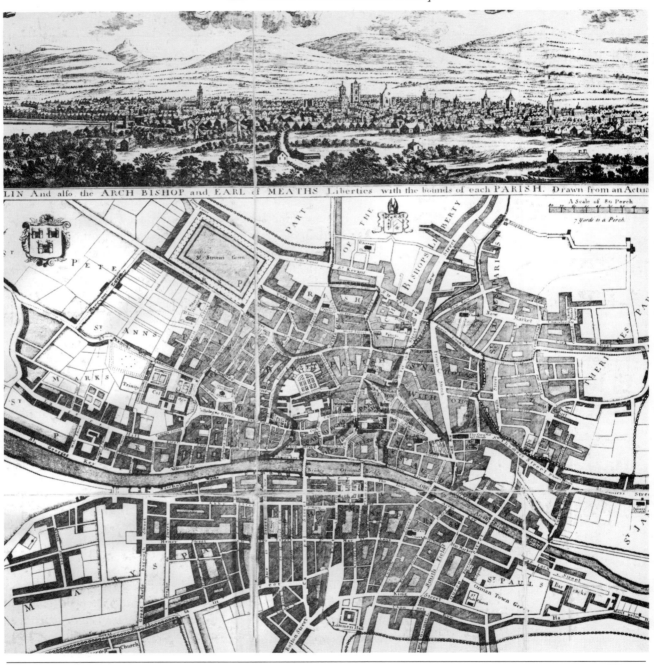

Do you live in the country, in a market town or in a larger town? How are people's everyday lives today affected by the kind of place they live in? Are the differences as great now as they were in the 1690s?

3 Before the Boyne: Who were the Irish?

A short answer might be: the people who lived in Ireland. In fact, there were many differences between them. Even people in the same kind of place such as a village or a sea-port could differ in their social position, language and religious beliefs. What were the main ways in which people in Ireland were similar and different?

The common people

In 1690 after the Battle of the Boyne, the English king offered pardon to many different groups.

A The king's pardon

". . . all poor Labourers, common Soldiers, Countrey Farmers, Plowmen and Cottiers whatsoever; As also all Citizens, Townsmen, Tradesmen and Artificers."

1 *Where did a cottier live?*

2 *What sort of work did an artificer do?*

What united all these different groups was the fact that they did not own land and collect rent from it. Because they were not landowners they were classed as common people, even though some of them were quite well-off. The common people made up nearly all the two million people living in Ireland at the end of the seventeenth century. About three-quarters of them were labourers on the land who were illiterate and knew little about anything beyond their own parish. On a higher social level were farmers who paid rent for their land to a landlord. They were about equal in rank to the craftsmen and small traders in towns.

The old landowners

A few landowning families had possessed their estates for centuries and were very proud of their family name, titles and traditions. These families were almost all Catholic. There was often a blood-relationship between them and their tenants. In some places the old custom of fostering went on, by which a tenant's child was brought up in the landowner's home.

A landowner was expected to be generous towards his tenants and other local common people such as craftsmen and traders. In return 'the commonalty' were expected to give loyalty to the local lord.

The number of these Catholic landowning families had been cut by two-thirds in the 1650s when Oliver Cromwell ruled England and Ireland. He had taken their houses and estates and given them to English families. Some Irish lords whose land had been taken lived in the woods as outlaws with armed followers and made a living by robbing and stealing. They were called Tories. Others stayed amongst their people. In the 1690s you could still find old landowners like the O'Sullivan Beare who was living on his family's old estate but 'in a cabin at the foot of the hill'. Such men still attracted the traditional loyalty of their former tenants.

B William King, Protestant Archbishop of Dublin, complains

". . . [the former landowners] have such an influence on the poor Tenants of their own Nation and Religion . . . that these tenants look on them still as a kind of Landlords; maintain them after a fashion in Idleness and entertain [provide for] them."

(From William King, *The State of the Protestants in Ireland*, 1691)

The new landowners

The new landowners were mostly from families who had been given land in Ulster by James I seventy years earlier, or in the rest of Ireland by Cromwell only forty years earlier. They were all Protestants of English or Scottish origin. Those in Ulster had some tenants of English or Scottish parentage but elsewhere almost all the tenants were Irish. Often the only link between the Catholic tenants and their Protestant landlord was the rent they paid him. Most of the new landlords were not members of ancient landowning families. The Irish poet, Dáibhidh Ó Bruadair (David O'Brudair) poured scorn on them, calling them ' . . . roughs formed from the dregs of each base trade . . . in the houses of the noblest chiefs, as proud and genteel as if sons of gentlemen'.

Which Churches did the Irish belong to?

The vast majority of the population were Catholics but they were mostly the landless people. The Catholic Church was banned by law but about a thousand parish clergy and eight hundred friars continued to work among the Catholic people. Bishops met in secret Synods to give guidance to their flocks. For example, Synods in the 1670s issued decrees to encourage sober behaviour at wakes and respect for the law.

The Church depended greatly on support from Catholics abroad. Men who wanted to train as priests had to go secretly to Irish colleges run by the Church in Europe. They risked their lives if they were caught and so did bishops and other priests making their way to Rome on church business.

C The Lord's Prayer in seventeenth-century Gaelic

3 *This was the first Catholic work printed in Irish. Why would it be printed in Antwerp?*

4 *How do you think it came to Ireland?*

(From a version printed in Antwerp)

Only the Protestant Church of Ireland was recognised by law. It was the sister-church of the Church of England and most of the wealthier families who had come from England since the sixteenth century belonged to it. They were landowners, wealthier farmers and well-to-do townspeople. Many such families had lived in Ireland for over a hundred years but in 1689 the Dean of Cork still described them as 'English gentlemen'.

In Ulster another form of Protestantism was strong. Many of the plantation farmers and some landowners were Presbyterians who had brought their beliefs from Scotland. The government allowed their Church or Kirk to practise its faith openly but it doubted their loyalty. Scottish Presbyterians had fought against Charles I in the English Civil War and Presbyterians in general were against churches being ruled by bishops and even states being ruled by kings.

What language did the Irish speak?

Most people spoke Gaelic and those who could write often wrote in it. The educated usually spoke English and Irish. The old gentry could speak to their tenants in Gaelic although they might use English among themselves. Even Dublin townspeople often used Irish as their first language. In the Ulster plantation areas English was often spoken by Protestants but Irish was still used by Catholics.

Some leaders of Protestant groups were in favour of encouraging Irish. A Quaker preacher, Katherine Norton, spoke in Irish to the people in Lisburn market place in 1678. Trinity College organised lectures in Irish and helped to publish the Bible in Irish. One of its provosts explained why:

D Promoting the Irish language

5 *Why did some Protestants want Bibles and preaching to be in Irish?*

6 *Do you agree that it is necessary for 'a free people' to have its own national language?*

" . . . methinks the Nation should make their Language triumphant . . . for why should a free people retain any marks of Slavery? Therefore perhaps, they'll endure the Scriptures in their own Tong, tho' not in ours."

(Dr Huntington, Provost of Trinity College, 1686)

Can you draw up rules for deciding a person's nationality which would apply to a) Ireland in the seventeenth century, b) Ireland today, c) All countries at any time?

4 Before the Boyne: Why was landowning so important?

What was so special about owning land that there was so much bitter argument and fighting about it?

How rich were landowners?

The size of estates varied. An example of a large one was the 64,000 acres owned by Viscount Dillon. This had been taken from him in Cromwell's time but was given back when Charles II became king in 1660. The value of estates varied also. The rents of the Earl of Clancarty, for example, came to £9,000 a year. Patrick Sarsfield owned a smaller estate near Dublin which brought in only £2,000 but at this time a farmer or merchant would feel quite well-off with £40 or £50 a year. Obviously a landowner's estate often covered many villages.

A Tenancies

1 Were there any advantages in the Kerry system of payment for the tenant or the landlord?

2 How many tenant farmers were there on the Duffyn estate?

3 How many other people paid rent to the landowner?

A1 *In 1674 Kerry Farmer Hugh McDermod Falvey paid £13 and:*

" . . . one barrel and a half of good merchantable barley malt, one fat winter hog or five shillings in lieu thereof, two fat summer sheep, one barrel of clean oats."

A2 *The Duffyn estate in Co Down included:*

" . . . 1,000 messuages [farmsteads] 1,600 cottages, 200 tofts [small plots] 10 watermills, 1,000 gardens, 15,000 acres of arable land, 1,000 acres of meadow, 1,000 acres of pasture, 10,000 acres of wood, 1,000 acres of moor, 1,000 acres of heath and furze, etc."

Some landowners made money from minerals. The Earl of Cork, in the 1670s had ten iron-smelting furnaces and more than twenty forges for making wrought iron, all using iron ore and charcoal from his own estate.

A landowner could also make money by selling the timber from the woods on his land. Lord Woodstock was given 135,800 acres which were taken from a Jacobite earl in 1691. Eight years later a commission of enquiry told the English House of Commons that he had sold £27,000 worth of timber. The commission complained about Protestant landlords who used their estates to make quick profits from timber.

B The 1699 commission of enquiry

4 Why might men like Lord Woodstock sell timber so cheaply?

" . . . so hasty have several of the Grantees of their Agents been . . . that vast numbers of trees have been cut and sold for not above 6 pence apiece."

What powers did landowners have?

A landowner's power did not come simply from his wealth. Landowning also carried privileges. In the counties, only landowners could vote to elect members of the Irish House of Commons and these MPs had to be landowners themselves.

C A Catholic landowner's house

The O'Brien family added an English-style house to the tower on the right.

5   *What does this suggest about the social position that some Catholic landowners aimed for?*

(Lemenagh Castle, County Clare)

The greater landowners, who were the nobility, were automatically members of the House of Lords without election. Landowners even had influence in the elections in the towns which had the right to send MPs to Parliament. In these towns, known as boroughs, only a few leading citizens had the vote. These men were often landowners because local landowners or members of their families usually owned property in the town.

The sons of landowners grew up learning the skills which fitted them for war. As boys they were taught to ride, shoot and use a sword. As young men they enjoyed the excitement and risks of hard riding in hunting parties. Many younger sons who would not inherit the family estate spent time abroad living on the pay of an officer in a European army. Most big country houses had an armoury with an assortment of muskets, pistols, swords and pikes. If war seemed likely, the landlord could recruit his tenants, their sons and labourers to form a regiment. The regiment would be known by his name and he paid for its weapons and equipment. In this way, in 1688, Gordon O'Neill of Tyrone raised O'Neill's Regiment of Infantry to serve James II while John Forward of Donegal formed a cavalry regiment to fight against him.

Most Protestant landowners had relatives in England and some of the old Catholic families had connections with English or Scottish gentry. These connections helped landowners to obtain direct news of what was going on in England and Scotland. Information and opinions then spread among other gentry. They often met for weddings, funerals and other family occasions or they might come together when they went to their town houses. The men were able to discuss politics and might agree on common action to support or oppose the government.

1   *If you were a landowner would you fight to keep your land? What else would you give up if you lost your land?*

2   *What kinds of people in the present day have the same sort of power and influence as landowners in the seventeenth century?*

5 Before the Boyne: Why did England want to rule Ireland?

Since the sixteenth century, English governments had tried hard to gain full control of Ireland, spending money to crush resistance and encouraging large numbers of English and Scots to become planters. What had England to gain from making Ireland a subject country?

A source of wealth?

Some European states ruled other countries to gain wealth. This could be achieved simply by mining for precious metals, for example as Spain did in Mexico and Peru. Another way was to make the inhabitants pay taxes. However, there were no gold or silver mines in Ireland, and the taxes raised rarely brought in enough money to cover the cost of governing Ireland itself. So the English government spent more than it gained.

Some states kept overseas colonies to supply them with goods which they could not produce at home. England, France and Holland all had colonies where they had granted land to planters who had slaves to grow tea, sugar and tobacco. But Ireland produced nothing which could not just as easily be grown in England. So Ireland was not valued in the same way as English colonies such as Barbados or Jamaica.

Colonial powers also saw their colonies as places where some of their own manufactured goods could be sold. Many English products such as woollen cloth and iron tools went to Barbados. But most people in Ireland grew their own food and wove their own cloth so they had little use for English manufactures.

A A prosperous English colony

(Bridgetown, the main port of Barbados in 1695)

1   *What signs are there that the colony was important to Britain's trade?*

2   *How would you describe the differences between a planter in a sugar-growing island such as Barbados and the planters in Ireland?*

The safety of England?

The south and west coasts of Ireland had many natural harbours and sheltered bays. They were too far from England's naval bases for her warships to keep a close eye on them. There was always a danger that one of England's enemies in Europe would land an army in Ireland, establish itself with Irish help and then launch an attack on England itself.

The sixteenth- and seventeenth-century plantations increased the number of people in Ireland who could be trusted to be loyal to England and stop attempts by the Irish to link up with England's enemies on the Continent. However, the fact that so many English and Scottish Protestant families were living in Ireland then became an added reason for the English government to keep control.

What did people in England think of Ireland?

In England the king and his advisers had to take notice of Parliament which represented the views of landowners and wealthy townspeople. These knew almost nothing about Ireland but they believed strongly that it 'belonged' to England, and that the Irish were lazy, violent and rebellious. They thought Ireland would never be of any benefit to England unless the people there changed their character or were removed altogether.

B An Irish Catholic bishop's view

3 Does Bishop O' Molony think the dislike was based on nationality or religion?

" . . . Any Englishman, Catholic or other, of what quality or degree soever alive . . . would as willingly see all Ireland over inhabited by English or whatsoever religion, as by the Irish."

(Bishop O'Molony from a letter quoted in William King, *The State of the Protestants in Ireland*, 1691)

C A Protestant archbishop's view

4 Why might you expect William King to be biased against Catholics?

5 What words does he use which suggest that he was biased?

" . . . [Ireland was] in a most flourishing condition . . . The Papists themselves, where Rancour, Pride or Laziness did not hinder them, lived happily, and a great number of them got considerable Estates [wealth] either by Traffick [trade] by the Law or by other Arts and Industry. There was a free Liberty of Conscience by connivance [not enforcing rules] tho' not by the Law."

(William King, Protestant Archbishop of Dublin)

The attitude of the Catholic Irish could not be expressed until 1689, when James II called a Parliament which voiced their opinions. They asked that the land confiscated by Cromwell should be returned and that the Catholic Church should have equal status with any other church, by law. On those terms they were willing to be ruled by an English king, though not by the English Parliament.

From the point of view of a seventeenth-century English person, list the reasons for:
a) continuing to rule Ireland
b) giving up rule over Ireland.

6 Europe in the 1680s: Rivalries and fears

For many centuries Ireland had links with the rest of Western Europe through the Catholic Church and through trade. In the late 1680s Ireland came to play a much more important part in the international politics of the Continent. What was the map of Western Europe like in 1685, and what were the ambitions, rivalries and fears of the rulers in Europe?

Germany

There was no single state with this name. The area known as Germany was made up of a hundred or so separate states, some little bigger than a town. Most states were ruled by a king, a prince or a duke, but three of the rulers were archbishops.

In theory all these rulers accepted the overlordship of the Holy Roman Emperor, whose personal territory was Austria. In fact they usually refused him any say in German affairs except when they wanted his protection against France. One reason for distrusting the Emperor was that he was a Catholic while many German rulers, especially in the north and northwest, were Protestants.

Austria

The Holy Roman Emperor ruled his own Austrian Empire which was much bigger than today's Austria. It included modern Czechoslovakia and parts of modern Hungary, Germany, Italy, Croatia and Slovenia. The Austrian emperors were members of the Habsburg family.

Spain

The kings of Spain came from another branch of the Habsburg family. They were Catholic and all the lands they ruled were Catholic. As well as Spain they ruled the southern half of Italy, the Spanish Netherlands (modern Belgium), and Franche Comté, between France and Switzerland.

The United Provinces

This country was also known as the Netherlands or Holland. It was made up of seven provinces. These had at one time been part of the Spanish Netherlands but they had won their freedom in 1609. Most Dutch people were Protestants. Holland, the largest province, was ruled by the Orange family. This name was taken from the district of Orange in southern France where the family came from. The United Provinces had a sort of parliament, or 'States'. In 1672 all the provinces had chosen William of Orange as their leader or 'stadhouder'.

France

France was the most powerful single state in Europe. It was ruled by Louis XIV who came to the throne as a boy and took over the government himself in 1661. Other European rulers envied the absolute control which Louis had over all aspects of life in France: the army, navy, trade, laws, and taxes.

Louis XIV was a Catholic and so were the vast majority of the French people. About two per cent of his subjects were Protestants, known as Huguenots. Up to 1685 they had been allowed freedom of worship by a decree, known as the Edict of Nantes. In 1685 Louis cancelled the Edict. Thousands of Huguenots emigrated to countries such as England and Ireland, the United Provinces and some of the Protestant states of Germany.

England

The kings of England were also kings of Scotland and Ireland. Most people in England and southern Scotland were Protestants. The people in the Scottish Highlands were mainly Catholic. In Ireland the vast majority were Catholics, except in Ulster, where there were many Protestants of Scottish descent. About two-thirds of the landowners in Ireland were Protestants.

The English Parliament was the strongest in Europe, because it had control over the collection of taxes. English kings had to be careful not to offend Parliament, yet they could often get their own way because Members of Parliament were not usually all of the same mind.

Europe overseas

Spain, France and England had overseas colonies and trading posts. Holland had fewer colonies but Dutch merchants had the world's biggest trading business, carrying goods back to Europe from every part of the world. Their success in this made other countries jealous. France, England and Holland had large fleets of warships to protect their merchant shipping.

A Europe in 1685

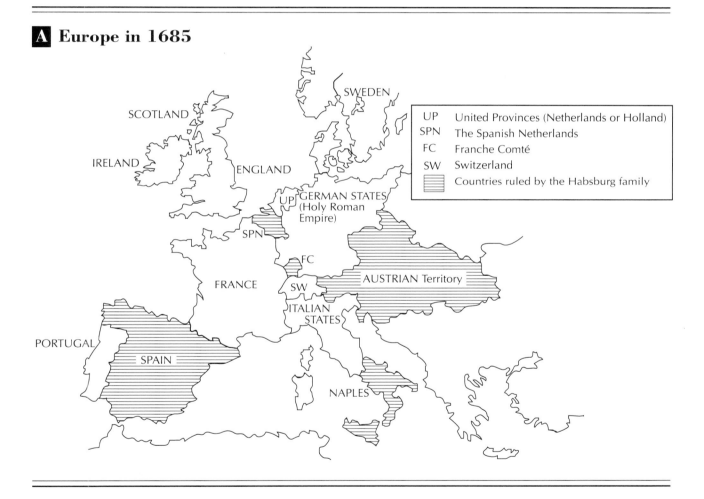

1 *Why might Louis XIV feel threatened by the Habsburg rulers?*

2 *Why might England, Holland and some German states be unfriendly towards France after 1685?*

3 *Why might England and Holland be a) enemies b) allies?*

4 *Why might France and England be a) enemies b) allies?*

7 Louis of France and William of Orange

In the 1670s and 1680s the rulers of France and the United Provinces built-up opposing alliances of European powers. What was the background to their rivalry? How was England drawn into the system of armed alliances?

Louis XIV's fears and ambitions

Louis was only twenty-three when he took over the government of France in 1661. He had good reason to feel that his kingdom would be more secure if it reached to the river Rhine which would be easier to defend. But Spain owned the Spanish Netherlands and Franche Comté, while other land between the Rhine and France was owned by German princes.

By 1685 it was France's neighbours who felt threatened. Louis had built a large, well-trained army and used it to take Franche Comté and part of the Spanish Netherlands. He took the city of Strasbourg and other small pieces of territory from German princes and forced them to allow his armies to march through their states whenever he wished. His brilliant military engineer, Vauban, was building massive fortresses in the newly-conquered lands and the French fleet of warships became the largest in Europe.

A Fighting in Europe from the 1660s to the 1690s

1   List the lands which Louis added to France.

2   What arguments could Louis give for his conquests?

3   How were the other European rulers likely to see Louis?

4   Which countries might William hope to pull into an alliance against France?

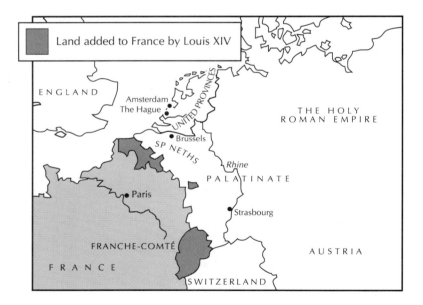

Land added to France by Louis XIV

ENGLAND

Amsterdam
The Hague

UNITED PROVINCES

Brussels

SP NETHS

Rhine

PALATINATE

THE HOLY ROMAN EMPIRE

Paris

Strasbourg

FRANCHE-COMTÉ

AUSTRIA

FRANCE

SWITZERLAND

William of Orange

William was born in 1650. His mother was a daughter of Charles I of England. In 1672, at the age of twenty-two, William became Captain-General of the Dutch army just when Louis XIV's army broke through the Spanish Netherlands and invaded the United Provinces.

William was inexperienced and his army was small. There was no natural barrier where they could stand to defend their country. As a last resort the Dutch broke holes in the dykes which kept the sea out of their low-lying land. The sea flooded homes and farms but the French advance was halted.

From this time on there was an intense hatred between William and Louis. Louis believed that if he could crush the United Provinces, France would grow rich on the wealth from Dutch trade and be able to dominate all Europe. William was determined that Louis should not get his own way. But to defeat Louis he needed an alliance of all the countries which feared French power.

How did England become involved?

When Louis invaded the United Provinces in 1672 he knew that the English navy or army would not come to the aid of the Dutch because he had made a secret treaty with Charles II of England. From that time William knew that success in fighting back against France depended on having England on his side. But that was not easy because England did not feel seriously threatened by Louis' conquests.

Charles II had favoured France partly because he was sympathetic to Catholics. He had no son so one day his brother James would be king of England. James had become a Catholic in 1668. In 1671 James's Protestant wife died leaving two daughters, Mary and Anne. Louis played a big part in finding James another wife, who was a Catholic Italian princess, Mary of Modena. He hoped that the marriage would encourage the future King James to side with Catholic France instead of Protestant Holland.

In England, one group of political leaders was in favour of being friendly towards the Dutch partly because of religion. In 1677 they persuaded Charles II to make an alliance with Holland. The alliance was sealed by a marriage between William of Orange and James's elder daughter Mary, who was a Protestant like her mother.

B The English Royal Family in 1677

5 *If James did not have a son, who would be ruler of England after his death?*

6 *Did William have any claims on the English throne?*

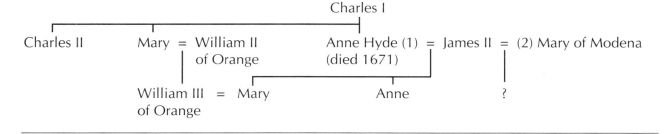

---

8 Why did James II lose England?

A Catholic king for England?

James II became king of England in February 1685. By Christmas 1688 he was a refugee in France. Why did this happen?

Most of the English were Protestants. The majority worshipped in the Church of England, which was the only faith recognised by law. A smaller number such as Presbyterians and Quakers were Dissenters, who were allowed to meet for prayers only in their own homes.

Protestants often believed that Catholics were dangerous enemies. They looked back to threats such as the Spanish Armada, the Gunpowder Plot and the Irish rebellion in 1641. Many people believed pamphlets which spread anti-Catholic propaganda in language like this: 'Fancy you behold troops of Papists . . . dashing little children's brains out against the walls, plundering your houses and cutting your own throats by the name of heretic dogs . . . imagine you see your father or your mother . . . tied to a stake in the midst of flames'.

James and Parliament

In 1678 Parliament passed the Test Act which forbade any Catholic to become an MP, a magistrate, judge, army officer, or hold any similar important position. When James became king he asked Parliament to abolish the Test Act, but they refused. James then used the right by which kings could excuse a person from obeying a certain law. He said that the Test Act did not apply to Catholic advisers and army officers. One was Richard Talbot who James put in charge of the army in Ireland. In November 1685 James closed Parliament without saying when he would call it again.

In 1687 James issued a Declaration of Indulgence, suspending all laws against Catholics and Dissenters. The king was now making and changing laws without taking any notice of Parliament. Many Englishmen thought he was trying to make himself an absolute ruler like Louis XIV. Above all, they were worried that James had doubled the size of his army although England was not at war.

A James II's army camped on Hounslow Heath

1 *Why might English people be alarmed by this scene?*

The crisis months, 1688

In 1687 James and Mary of Modena had been married for fifteen years, but had no children. People were looking forward to the day when James would die and his Protestant daughter, Mary, would become queen. Then in the spring of 1688 news came that James's wife was pregnant. If she had a son he would be next in line for the throne. The hope of an heir made James more confident. He issued another Declaration of Indulgence and ordered it to be read out in every church. Seven bishops refused, saying that James had no right to change laws except by agreement of Parliament. James had them arrested and put on trial.

On 10 June Mary of Modena gave birth to a son, but there was little public rejoicing. Some people even started a rumour that the baby had been smuggled into the palace in a warming-pan, and was not James's son at all.

On 30 June the judges at the trial of the seven bishops declared them not guilty. The Governor of York wrote that 'The streets were so crammed with cheering people that it looked like a little rebellion'. On the same day Admiral Herbert left London for Holland, disguised as a fisherman. He took with him a letter from seven political leaders, addressed to William of Orange.

B The English letter

2 *What was this letter suggesting to William?*

3 *Is there any evidence that William was expecting it?*

"Your Highness may be assured there are nineteen parts of twenty of the people throughout the kingdom, who are desirous of change, and who, we believe, would willingly contribute to it . . . We who subscribe [sign] this will not fail to attend your Highness upon your landing and to do all that lies in our power to prepare others to be in . . . readiness."

In fact William's agents had been discussing the possibility with some English politicians since 1685. But now he had to see if it would be safe to take an army to England. In September William heard that the French had invaded the Palatinate which was a place three hundred miles away from the Netherlands. At once he prepared to sail for England and sent manifestos on ahead to explain why he was coming.

C William's manifestos

4 *What impression was William trying to create in these manifestos?*

"The prince had no other design in this expedition but for the good of England and the preservation of the Protestant religion."

"Our expedition is intended for no other design but to have a free and lawful Parliament assembled as soon as possible."

William and his army landed in south-west England on 5 November. The English did not rush to support him but few were eager to fight for James. James himself could not decide what to do. In the end he could only think of one plan; to flee to France. William kept his promise to call a Parliament. It proclaimed that William and Mary were jointly king and queen.

1 *Now that William was king of England as well as stadhouder of the Netherlands, how would it help him to defeat Louis?*

2 *What if : a) James had not had a son in 1688?*
b) Louis had launched an attack on Holland in September 1688?

9 What was James II's policy in Ireland?

James II became king of Ireland as well as England and Scotland in February 1685. How was Ireland affected by having a ruler who was sympathetic towards Catholics? In November 1688 James lost the throne of England and Scotland but was still king of Ireland. What effect did this have on Ireland?

What changes did James make before 1688?

In 1685 James put his Catholic friend, Richard Talbot, in command of the Irish army, which was almost entirely Protestant. Talbot immediately began to appoint Catholic officers and recruit Catholics as soldiers. By September 1686 about two-thirds of the army were Catholics. However, James took no action against the Protestant landowners who had been given estates by Cromwell. Talbot wanted to give the lands back to Catholic families but James had no wish to upset the landowning classes.

Early in 1687, James made Talbot Lord Lieutenant of Ireland with the title of Earl of Tyrconnell. This gave him much more power in the country, to the alarm of the Protestants.

A English comments on Tyrconnell's rule

1 *What do these extracts tell you about the effect on Protestants of putting Tyrconnell in charge of Ireland?*

A1 "Lord Tyrconnell gone to succeed the lord lieutenant in Ireland to the astonishment of all sober [sensible] men, and to the evident ruin of the protestants in that kingdom."
(From the diary of John Evelyn)

A2 "We hear that many of the most considerable [important] persons of Ireland will come away . . . there are thousands coming away already."
(Sir William Petty, 18 January 1687)

Tyrconnell lost no time in carrying out James's policies. He appointed Catholics as judges and sheriffs of counties. He changed the rules about town councils to allow Catholics to become councillors. It was clear that when an Irish Parliament was next called most MPs would be Catholics. There were now very few Protestants left in the army. Tyrconnell added to its size and sent some regiments to England to strengthen the king's position there.

James II in Ireland after 1688

When news came that James had fled to France, Tyrconnell was in firm control and Catholics held nearly all key positions. Legally, James was still king of Ireland and he might still win back the English throne if Louis XIV helped him. These were good reasons why even the Protestants in Ulster did not rush to give public backing to William, the new king of England.

In March 1689 James took the first step to recover the English crown with French help. He sailed from France and landed at Kinsale with a few French officers. An army of three thousand French soldiers followed a few weeks later. After James had landed, elections were held for a Parliament which met in May 1689. All but six MPs were Catholic.

B James landing at Kinsale, March 1689

2 *Why are all the guns firing?*

3 *How does the artist bring out the fact that James was a Catholic?*

C Letter to Louis XIV from a French officer

4 *What reasons does d'Avaux give to explain why James was welcomed in Cork?*

"arriva   hier   au soir à Kork que   les acclamations
arrived yesterday evening at Cork where the rejoicings

y on esté grande . . .quoyquil   y ait   beaucoup de huguenots
were   great . . . although there are   many   Protestants

ils   ont esté desarmez et   le nombre des catholiques est bien
they had been disarmed and the number of   Catholics   is much

superieur."
higher.

In May 1689, the new Catholic MPs passed laws to remove Ireland from English control. England's Parliament and law courts were to have no authority in Ireland. There were to be no laws favouring one religion. Each person was to pay tithe (church tax) to his own Church.

James was unhappy at all this because it would weaken his position if he ever again became king of England. However, he had to accept because he needed help in recovering the English throne. One Irish MP put the point bluntly: 'If your Majesty will not fight for our rights we will not fight for yours.'

Most MPs belonged to families who had lost some or all of their land. They went against James's wishes and passed an Act of Attainder against more than 2,400 Protestant landowners who had left Ireland when Tyrconnell became Lord Lieutenant. The Act declared them guilty of treason and said the land was to be confiscated and shared among Catholics who had lost estates under Cromwell.

Parliament had created a Catholic supremacy in Ireland but they would have to defend it against the armies of William. The Protestants of Londonderry and Iniskillen had been keeping a foothold for him in Ulster ever since 1688. In August 1689 William sent one of his generals, Marshal Schomberg, with an army which landed at Carrickfergus.

Irish Catholics spoke of James II 'With his one shoe English and his one shoe Irish'. What did they mean by this? How strong was this trust in James?

10 Why did Ulster resist James II?

Why did the Protestants in Ulster decide to give their loyalty to William of Orange, the new king of England? What difference did it make to James's hope of success?

The settlers in Ulster

There were about as many Protestants living in Ulster as in all the other provinces added together. Over the rest of the country the Protestants were mostly landlords and a few of their wealthier tenants. In Ulster whole communities – landowners, farmers, labourers, and tradesmen – were all Protestants. In the other provinces almost all the Protestants were Church of Ireland members. In Ulster most were Presbyterians of Scottish descent.

Until James II tried to change the law, the Church of Ireland was the only one recognised by the government. Its clergy, however, often neglected their work, as a leading nobleman complained to the Archbishop of Canterbury: 'Very few of the clergy reside on their cures [parishes] but employ pitiful curates; which necessitates the people to look after [turn to] a romish priest or non-conformist [Presbyterian] preacher; and there are plenty of both.'

The Presbyterian ministers lived among their people and often worked a small farm to make a living as well as preaching and visiting their congregations. They had to follow a strict course of training and pass many tests to become qualified. The leading men in each congregation were called elders. They could summon anyone before them for sins such as 'profaning the Sabbath' or 'being scandalously overtaken with drink'. If the sinners refused to mend their ways they could be 'declared to be none of our Communion'. The rest of the community would then have no more contact with them. Elders also collected money for the poor and helped to provide schooling.

1 Why might Presbyterian ministers be more respected than the Church of Ireland clergy?

2 How did their outlook and organisation strengthen the Presbyterian communities of Ulster?

The separate Presbyterian congregations throughout Ulster kept in touch through regular meetings of ministers and elders. Each felt that it would get help from the others in times of trouble but that everyone else was against them. Their Church was not recognised by law and the Church of Ireland obstructed them in every possible way. They saw the Catholic Irish as dangerous enemies, kept down only by the power of the king.

How did the Ulster settlers react to James II?

The settlers became very alarmed when Tyrconnell began to appoint Catholics to key positions and build up a Catholic Irish army. His policy revived memories of the 1641 uprising which began in Ulster where many settlers were killed. Until 1685, when James became king, they had felt secure because of the government's restrictions on Catholics in public life and the army.

When Tyrconnell had become Lord Lieutenant many Protestant landowners had thought it safer to go to England but ordinary Protestants, especially the Ulster Presbyterians, could not afford to do this. In Ulster there were enough to stand their ground and defend themselves. When the people of Enniskillen were told they must not arm without the king's permission, they asked 'are we to sit still and let ourselves be butchered?' The new threat united members of the Church of Ireland and Presbyterians.

A How the English viewed Tyrconnell

3 *Which figure is Tyrconnell? What is he doing?*

4 *How does the card illustrate Protestant fears?*

(An English playing card of about 1689)

Why did the War of the Two Kings begin in Ulster?

In November 1688 Tyrconnell sent three Irish regiments to England to help James against William. To do this he had to remove the garrison of Londonderry to replace them with a newly-formed regiment. It was nearly three weeks before the new troops arrived. In the meantime the city council had to decide whether to remain loyal to James and let the new garrison in or whether to keep control of the city themselves. Many feared for their lives if they let in Tyrconnell's soldiers. Yet, if they refused and James remained king, he might hang them as rebels. On 7 December they still had not come to a decision when the new regiment came in sight. At the last moment thirteen apprentices rushed to the city gates and shut them. Tyrconnell's troops had to withdraw.

The news from England in the winter of 1688–9 encouraged the Protestants in Ulster. James had fled to France. William was king and had promised to send help. In March, however, James came to Ireland with French advisers. He sent part of his army, led by Richard Hamilton, to Ulster. On 14 March it overwhelmed a Protestant force at Dromore in County Down. This was the first serious fighting in *Cogadh an Dá Rí* – the War of the Two Kings. The sides took the kings' names and became known as Williamites and Jacobites (from Jacobus, the Latin for James).

After their defeat at Dromore, the Williamites gathered their men in two strongholds, Enniskillen and Londonderry. The Jacobites' main aim was to get control of Londonderry. If they captured it William would not be able to land troops and Protestant resistance would collapse. James could use the harbour to ship an Irish army to Scotland. There he would be supported by the Highland Scots who had refused to accept William.

1 *Imagine you are a member of the city council. Discuss with the other councillors whether to admit Tyrconnell's troops.*

2 *Why was Londonderry so important to the outcome of the war?*

11 The siege of Derry

On 15 April Richard Hamilton led the Jacobite army across the river Finn about thirty miles from Londonderry. On the same day English ships with troops and supplies sailed up Lough Foyle. The siege of Derry was about to begin. Many descriptions of it tell a simple story of Protestants holding out against great odds until help arrived. What really happened at Derry in 1689?

The siege begins

Robert Lundy, the Military Governor, argued that even with the troops who had arrived resistance would be hopeless. The city walls were weak, food supplies were short and the place was overcrowded with old people, women and children from the surrounding countryside. He was opposed by some of the city council, who accused him of being cowardly or even a secret Jacobite. However, the commander of the English fleet accepted Lundy's view that his troops were bound to be defeated if they joined in the defence of Derry. He sailed his ships away.

1 *Lundy's effigy was later burned each year on the anniversary of the siege. Why was this? Is Lundy's reputation as a traitor a fair one?*

Lundy was now deeply unpopular and no one tried to stop him when he fled, leaving the city to its fate. Two men were chosen to take charge of the defence. They were Major Henry Baker and the Rev George Walker, a Church of Ireland clergyman. On 18 April James II appeared with his army at Bishop's Gate. He was met by ragged firing from the walls and shouts of 'No surrender'. He returned to Dublin, leaving Hamilton to get control of the city.

The siege continues

Hamilton repeatedly promised the Protestants that if they surrendered they would be allowed to keep their land and property. As time dragged on, such offers became more tempting. On 13 July a parley took place between Hamilton and delegates from Derry. Hamilton wanted an immediate surrender but the Protestants asked for a delay, to make sure that James II himself agreed to the terms, and the talks came to nothing. Hamilton offered similar terms to any individuals who left the city and went back to their homes in the countryside. About 10,000 people accepted his offer, and were not harmed.

2 *How true are these statements?*
a) No Protestant would ever accept James as king.
b) Catholics would kill Protestants if they got the chance.

3 *What were the military advantages and disadvantages on each side?*

Hamilton had around 10,000 men while the armed defenders numbered some 7,000. About one-third of the Jacobites were cavalry who could not be used in siege warfare. Many of the infantry were recent recruits, partly trained and poorly armed. For the first six weeks Hamilton had no cannon large enough to do much damage to the weak city walls. Most of the Williamites were not trained soldiers either, but they did have about twenty cannon. There were several minor battles when the Jacobites advanced too close and the defenders sallied out to drive them away, but there was no all-out attack.

Starvation

The Jacobites were able to prevent any food from entering the city over land, and early in June a French military engineer built a boom of timber, chains and ropes across the river Foyle to stop supplies by sea. At the end of June General Rosen, a French officer, took command from Hamilton. He decided to make the defenders' food problem worse by forcing more people into the city. Over a thousand country people were rounded up and left outside the gates without food or shelter.

The Williamites refused to let them in and threatened to hang all their Jacobite prisoners in retaliation so Rosen let the refugees go home. On hearing of this incident, James dismissed him and reappointed Hamilton.

A The Protestant Archbishop of Dublin's account

4 *Rosen appears to have been very cruel. How would he have defended his action?*

" . . . the very Papist Officers that executed [carried out] the thing, confest that it was the most dismal sight they had ever seen, and that the cries of the poor People seem'd to be still [always] in their ears."

(From William King, *The State of the Protestants in Ireland*, 1691)

Early in June English ships appeared in Lough Foyle but the commander, Major-General Kirke, was advised by his council-of-war not to attack.

Towards the end of July the garrison's weekly rations were down to a pound of oatmeal and a pound of tallow per man. Ordinary citizens had to buy what they could at extremely high prices.

By 28 July Walker estimated that there was only two days' food left. There were only about 3,000 fit men left to defend the walls. Thousands of the citizens were dead, victims of disease or starvation or killed in the fighting or by cannon-fire. The besiegers had also lost thousands, mostly from disease. They were not well supplied with food once all the local resources were used up, and they had little or no shelter.

B Londonderry at the time of the siege

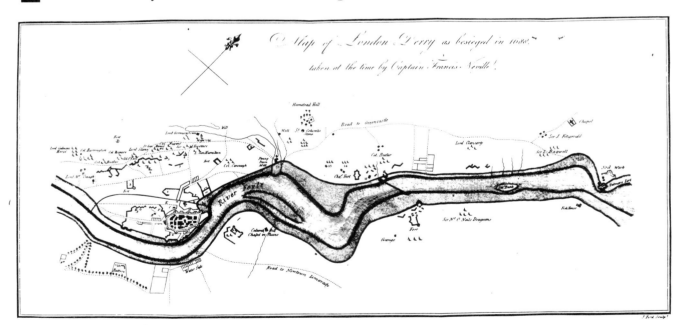

(From a plan drawn by Francis Neville, member of the City Corporation)

5 *In which direction is the sea?*

6 *The names of the Jacobite commanders are given. What does their position tell you about the difficulties of the people in the city?*

7 *Where is the boom? Why was this a good place to put it?*

8 *Would you prefer to have been in the besieging army or in the city (leaving out what your political views might have been)?*

C Advice to Kirke

9 *Why did the boom make it too risky for the English fleet to go forward to Londonderry?*

" . . . the Boume, which if not broke by our attempt, the breadth of the river is so narrow as that the ship will certainly run ashoare. [The enemy would then capture] so many great guns with our stores of war and victuals, which if they had, they would certainly make a more formall attaque upon the town of Londonderie . . . "

The siege raised

Kirke and his fleet came back to the Foyle on 21 July, but had to wait for a north wind until 28 July at six o'clock in the evening. Then two transport ships headed for the boom. When the first ship, the *Mountjoy*, rammed the boom she rebounded and ran aground stern first. A troop of Jacobite cavalry galloped up but were driven off, and she refloated on the rising tide. Meanwhile a boatload of sailors reached the boom and one of them hacked through the cable, so that at the second attempt the *Mountjoy* broke through. She and the *Phoenix* were then towed up-river. They tied up at the quay and began unloading beef, flour, meal and other supplies. Three days later the besiegers withdrew. Shortly afterwards the Williamites besieged in Enniskillen came out and defeated the Jacobites at Newtownbutler. William's supporters now controlled most of Ulster so he could use it as a base to advance on Dublin.

D Food and prices under siege

In peacetime a labourer's family might live on 5s (shillings) a week (1s = 5p). There were twelve old pence (d) in a shilling.

Horse-flesh 1s 8d

Quarter of a dog 5s 6d
(fattened by eating the bodies of the slain Irish)

A dog's head 2s 6d

A cat 4s 6d

A rat 1s 0d

A mouse 6d

A quart of meal when found 1s 0d

(From George Walker, *A True Account of the Siege of Londonderry*, 1689)

Several people kept diaries during the siege. Imagine you are one of the citizens and write a few days' entries; or write a letter describing your experiences during these events.

2 The armies of William and James

A fortnight after the relief of Derry an English army led by Marshal Schomberg landed at Carrickfergus. Through the winter of 1689–90 they strengthened the hold on Ulster. In June 1690 William himself arrived with a larger army, aiming to take Dublin. The Jacobites fell back until they reached the Boyne, where they hoped to block William's advance. If there was to be a battle, which king had the best chance of winning?

How was William's army made up?

Most of William's troops were well-trained, well-equipped and led by experienced officers. He had about 35,000 men. Fewer than half were English. There was a very large force of Dutch troops, including William's own horse-guards and his foot-guards, called the Blue Guards from the colour of their uniforms. One regiment was from Brandenburg (in Germany) and eleven were from Denmark. Both Brandenburg and Denmark were members of the alliance against Louis XIV. There were Huguenot soldiers who had left France because of religious persecution. William also had the help of the Eniskilleners from Ulster.

A William's Eniskilleners

1 *Why were there soldiers from so many different countries in William's army?*

"The sight of their thin little nags and the wretched dress of their riders, half-naked with sabre and pistols hanging from their belts, looked like a horde of Tartars."

(George Story, chaplain with William's army)

William's foot-soldiers were of two types, musketeers and pikemen. Most of the musketeers were armed with matchlock muskets about 1.6m long and weighing about 4.5kg. The musket fired a lead ball and had a range of 400–450m. The powder was ignited with the glowing end of the match – a length of cord treated with saltpetre to make it burn away slowly. It took several minutes to load and fire and this left the musketeers open to attack by cavalry. This was why musketeers and pikemen fought in supporting sections. The pikemen held 4.8m long poles, tipped with a steel spike, to hold off the enemy cavalry while their comrades re-loaded.

The Blue Guards and the Danish infantry were equipped with faster-firing flintlock muskets, in which the powder was set off by a spark. The Blue Guards also had plug bayonets. These had a wooden handle which could be fitted into the muzzle of the musket, turning it into a kind of short pike.

Horse-soldiers were either dragoons or true cavalry. Dragoons were mounted infantry who rode into or out from battle, but normally fought on foot. Cavalrymen made charges on horseback and were armed with sabres and a brace of flintlock pistols.

William had 36 field-guns and twelve siege-guns for use against fortified towns. The field-guns fired iron cannon-balls to unnerve the enemy before the cavalry and infantry moved forward to attack. The siege-guns were hauled by teams of sixteen horses, but they were too heavy for battlefield use.

What was James's army like?

James had about 6,000 French and 19,000 Irish soldiers. The French were commanded by the Comte de Lauzun, a nobleman without much military experience. Before 1685 no Catholics were allowed in the Irish army, so most of the officers and men had very little training or experience. The Irish treasury was short of money to buy weapons and other military supplies. As in many armies of the time, some officers kept money which should have been used to pay and equip their men. The soldiers had to live as best they could, often by stealing. The Jacobites had only twelve field-guns.

Louis XIV had supplied some muskets for the Irish army, but they were faulty and unreliable and there were not enough. The cavalry were in better shape because horse-soldiers were from a higher social class and had the first choice of uniforms and equipment.

B A French view of James's army

2 *How does the Count say that the Irish infantry were unlikely to be much use in battle, but might be made into good soldiers?*

" . . . armées seulement de bastons, dont quelques uns
    armed only with staves, some of which

ont du fer au bout en manier de piques . . .
are tipped with iron like pikes . . .

    sont tres bien faits, mais ils ne sont ny
[the men] are very well built, but they are neither

dissiplinez, ny armez, et du surplus sont degrands voleurs."
disciplined nor armed, and most of them are great thieves.

(The Comte d'Avaux reporting to Louvois, the French War Minister)

C Flintlock musket

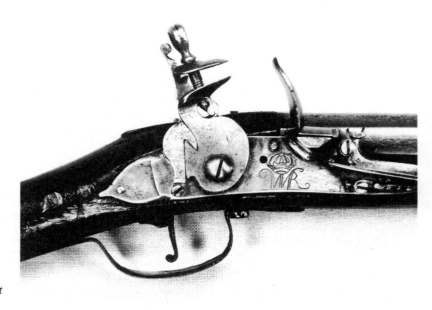

3 *Why would this weapon be difficult to aim accurately? Notice the piece of flint held in the jaws of the cock. What do the initials WR stand for?*

Make two columns, headed 'Williamite army' and 'Jacobite army'. Compare the two, using the following side headings: Size, Training, Experience, Weapons. Add other side headings if you like.

13 The Battle of the Boyne

On Monday 30 June William's army took up position facing the Jacobites who were camped across the Boyne. They had chosen this position to stop the Williamites crossing the Boyne at the ford at Oldbridge. That evening the gunners exchanged cannon-fire. James narrowly escaped being hit and William was wounded slightly in the shoulder. Both kings knew that the next day could settle the future for themselves, their countries and the war in Europe.

A The Battle of the Boyne

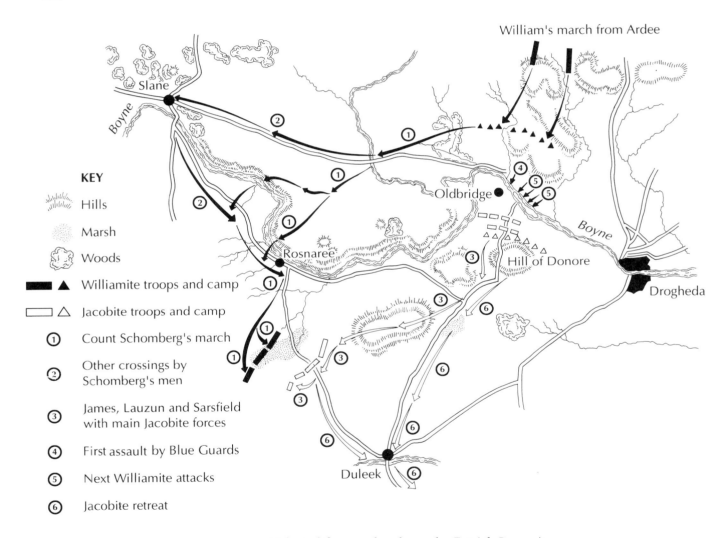

(Adapted from a plan drawn by Patrick Leeson)

KEY

- Hills
- Marsh
- Woods
- ■ ▲ Williamite troops and camp
- ▢ △ Jacobite troops and camp
- ① Count Schomberg's march
- ② Other crossings by Schomberg's men
- ③ James, Lauzun and Sarsfield with main Jacobite forces
- ④ First assault by Blue Guards
- ⑤ Next Williamite attacks
- ⑥ Jacobite retreat

The first moves

At about two o'clock in the morning of 1 July the Williamite drums beat the call to arms. As a badge for the day every man had to wear a bunch of green leaves. On the Jacobite side they wore a piece of white cloth. William sent 8,000 troops led by Count Schomberg (Marshal Schomberg's son) along the road to their right. Under cover of the dense morning mist they were to cross the Boyne upstream from the Jacobite camp at Oldbridge.

Most of Schomberg's men crossed at the ford at Rosnaree which was guarded by only 480 Irish dragoons. They were all across by half-past nine. James thought that the rest of William's army would follow and either attack Oldbridge from the rear or march straight to Dublin along the Slane–Duleek road. James and Lauzun with the French troops together with Sarsfield and most of the Irish army moved to block the road. Schomberg's men took several hours to reach the Jacobite position. When they did, neither side was able to attack the other because of the boggy ground with many streams and gullies between them.

The battle at Oldbridge

The move to block Count Schomberg meant that only five or six thousand Jacobite troops, led by Tyrconnell, were still at Oldbridge. At about 11 a.m. William judged that it was time to cross the ford. With fifes and drums playing the Williamite march, *Lillebulero*, the Dutch Blue Guards waded across waist-deep with hardly a break in formation. Tyrconnell's infantry kept up steady musket–fire and fought them hand-to-hand but the Guards gradually forced the Irish back.

Tyrconnell had to break this Williamite foothold before others could cross. The obvious way was to use cavalry, as the Guards did not include any pikemen. The Duke of Berwick led a charge of a thousand Irish troopers, but the Guards quickly formed up in squares, fixed bayonets and met them with a bristling wall of steel. The Irish charged again and again and the squares began to break, but more Williamites were already crossing, firing as they came, and the Irish cavalry had to fall back.

About the same time the Danish infantry crossed further down the river. An hour or two later, more Williamites got across and William himself followed with his Horse Guards. The Irish cavalry were now outnumbered and the men and horses were tired.

B Williamite troops gaining a foothold in Oldbridge

(From an etching by R. de Hodge, published in 1690)

1   *Why did William delay his main attack until 11 o'clock?*

2   *When did Tyrconnell use cavalry and why did this plan not succeed?*

The Jacobites give way

The Irish musketeers had used up all their powder and shot, so a man could only use his sword or hold his musket by the barrel and use it like a club. The cavalry were reduced to about a thousand. They tried to make a stand on the hill of Donore but more Williamites were streaming across the Boyne. The battle was lost.

Some time after 2 p.m. James was told that his army at Oldbridge was shattered. He decided to retreat to Dublin, leave his Irish kingdom in the care of Tyrconnell and return to France.

His troops had stood in battle order all day under the blazing sun. They were on edge from the strain of waiting and could guess what had happened at Oldbridge. As they hurried along they were thrown into disarray by troopers galloping headlong from the battlefield.

C Captain Stevens on the Jacobites' retreat

3   *What 'danger' could Stevens see in the soldiers 'dispersing'?*

"What few men I could see I called to, no command being of force, begging them to stand together and repair to their colours, the danger being in dispersing, but all in vain, some throwing away their arms, others even their coats and shoes to run lighter."

The end of the day

Around five o'clock some fugitives began to straggle into Dublin. James himself reached the city at 10 p.m. The Irish cavalry rode in about midnight.

On the south bank of the Boyne the smell of gunsmoke lingered in the evening mist. Bodies of men and horses lay scattered over the field, already stripped of anything worth taking. The wounded, Williamite or Jacobite, moaned with pain or cried out in delirium. Injuries from musket-fire, pike thrusts and sabre cuts were often beyond medical treatment. A regimental surgeon dealt first with officers, while the common soldiers tended to their wounded comrades as best they could.

The Williamites lost about five hundred men. About a thousand Jacobites were killed and several hundred taken prisoner. These were disarmed and then turned loose. Otherwise they would have to be fed and troops taken from combat duty to guard them.

Within a couple of days, the Williamites had occupied Dublin. James was on his way to France while his army was on the march towards Limerick.

1   *Write down incidents in the battle which show the importance of: military training and discipline; better weapons; having larger numbers of soldiers.*

2   *Discuss, as Jacobite officers, why you lost the battle, and what should have been done to win.*

3   *Imagine you are a soldier who was in the battle. Give your personal account of it. Remember you could not see the whole area, only what was going on around you.*

14 From the Boyne to Limerick

James II and the Jacobites were defeated at the Battle of the Boyne on 1 July 1690 but more than a year passed before the Jacobite army finally surrendered at Limerick. What happened during that time? How were James's Irish supporters able to keep up their resistance for so long?

James leaves Ireland

The Battle of the Boyne was celebrated in Europe as a great victory for William and his allies over Louis XIV. The Dutch were delighted. In Austria and Spain thanksgiving services were held. The Pope, who resented Louis' treatment of the Catholic Church in France, was pleased. It was only in Ireland that the battle was seen as a victory for Protestants over Catholics.

James lost no time in getting away from Ireland. Before he left Dublin he spoke to the Lord Mayor and Corporation.

A James on the Battle of the Boyne

"Here I had an army that was loyal enough, but that they wanted [lacked] true courage to stand by me at the critical minute. Gentlemen, I am now a second time necessitated to provide for my own safety . . . I advise you all to make the best terms you can for yourselves. I desire you all to be kind to the Protestant inhabitants and not to injure them or this city; for though I at present quit it , yet I do not quit for my interest in it."

1 *Do you agree with the reason James gave for his defeat?*

2 *'A second time' – when was the first time that James had to provide for his own safety?*

3 *What did James mean by saying that he did not give up his interest in Dublin?*

The first siege of Limerick, August 1690

Most of the Jacobite forces were now gathered at Limerick. Tyrconnell and Lauzun, the French commander, wanted to come to terms with William but Sarsfield and the Irish officers decided to fight on. Lauzun refused to risk his French troops in a hopeless defence of Limerick so he took them to Galway.

The Williamites easily subdued most of Leinster and Munster, and reached Limerick on 8 August. The fortifications were very weak and there were no French troops in the city. William was sure that as soon as his siege-guns began to fire the defence would collapse. These heavy cannon were still on their way, several miles behind the Williamite camp.

Sarsfield took a detachment of cavalry and made his way round the Williamite lines. They found the siege-train encamped for the night, blew up the guns and returned safely to Limerick.

William still had field-guns and after a few weeks these battered a gap in the wall. On 27 August a regiment of grenadiers stormed the breach. The men and women of the city joined in the defence, supporting the musket-fire of the garrison with a hail of stones. The Williamites fell back and two days later William called off the siege.

It was now about ten weeks since William had come to Ireland and he was anxious to return to England. Some political leaders there were not totally loyal to him, as they still half-expected that James might recover the throne. William also wanted to visit Holland and plan his next moves against Louis XIV. He sailed for Bristol, leaving his Dutch general, Ginkel, in command in Ireland.

Ginkel advances: June and July 1691

Soon after William's return to England, Lauzun and Tyrconnell went to France with the French regiments, leaving Sarsfield with only enough men to hold Limerick and the country west of the Shannon. In May 1691 a French fleet delivered arms and supplies to Limerick. There were no French troops, but an experienced general, St Ruth, was sent by James to take command.

Ginkel now advanced towards the Shannon and reached Athlone on 19 June. He easily got control of the town east of the river but was held back at the bridge. A fierce battle went on there until the end of June, when Ginkel got across at a ford. St Ruth had to withdraw to Aughrim, where he drew up his army to block Ginkel's advance on Galway.

B The Williamite wars

4 What difficulties did William have in trying to capture Limerick?

5 What other reasons did he have for returning to England?

6 Why did Louis XIV not send more French troops to Limerick?

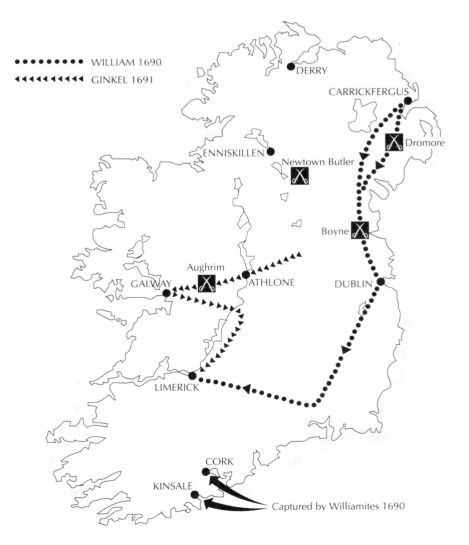

●●●●●●●● WILLIAM 1690
◀◀◀◀◀◀◀◀ GINKEL 1691

DERRY
CARRICKFERGUS
Dromore
ENNISKILLEN
Newtown Butler
Boyne
Aughrim
GALWAY ATHLONE DUBLIN
LIMERICK
CORK
KINSALE
Captured by Williamites 1690

Ginkel was under pressure from William to finish the war as quickly as possible so that troops could be transferred to the Netherlands. His army reached Aughrim on 12 July and he decided to attack at once, at about five o'clock in the evening.

The Williamites had to advance across a bog to reach the Irish who were well protected behind earthworks. Each wave of infantry was driven back, but some cavalry managed to cross.

The Irish were now being attacked from the side as well as the front. St Ruth was killed by a cannon-shot so they had no one to give orders to deal with the new threat. As darkness fell their resistance collapsed. About four thousand Irish troops were killed. Sarsfield led most of the survivors to Limerick. Ginkel marched on to Galway which surrendered on 21 July.

Ginkel and his victorious army reached Limerick on 14 August. Soon the city was being bombarded daily by his cannon. English warships blocked the river on the seaward side so Limerick was now completely cut off and supplies of food and ammunition were already very low.

Sarsfield realised that he would have to surrender in the end. Ginkel was aware that the siege was tying down an army which William would be glad to have in the Netherlands. Both leaders saw that they could gain more by coming to terms instead of fighting on. They agreed a cease-fire and the treaty was finally signed on 3 October. A few days later a French fleet arrived in the Shannon with food and military supplies.

The second siege of Limerick, September 1691

1 *How did the fighting between William and Louis XIV affect the war in Ireland?*

2 *It appears that William was prepared to spend more money and use more troops than Louis XIV to secure control of Ireland. Why do you think this was?*

3 *Select and describe a few occasions when chance played an important part in the course of events.*

5 The Treaty of Limerick

When Limerick was besieged for the second time the Williamite general Ginkel was in a hurry to end the fighting. William needed his army elsewhere in Europe and he was ready to offer terms of surrender to Sarsfield. What were the terms of this treaty and why did Catholics later call it the 'broken Treaty'?

What kind of a treaty was it?

The treaty was made between the commanders of the two armies. It was completed and signed within a few days. It was not like a treaty between two countries negotiated by skilled diplomats. Because of this, it cannot be seen as a permanent peace treaty between William and Louis XIV, or between William and James II, or between England and Ireland.

The treaty included some points about the Irish army. These are called the Military Articles. The terms which concerned civilians are known as the Civil Articles.

The Military Articles

1 *Why did Ginkel offer terms of surrender to Sarsfield?*

2 *What did William gain by the treaty and what did James II and Louis XIV gain?*

3 *Do you think these terms were fair?*

In the seventeenth century, when soldiers surrendered, they were usually given the choice of joining the victorious army, going home, or joining another country's army. Ginkel agreed that the Irish troops who surrendered could go home, or accept service in the armies of William, or join the armies of Louis XIV. About two thousand returned to their homes, promising to accept William as king. One thousand joined William's army. About 14,000 decided to join the French army.

A few days after the treaty was signed a French fleet arrived. It had been sent to bring supplies to the city but it was now used to take about half the garrison to France. The remainder sailed later from Cork on ships provided by William. Those who went to France were forbidden to return to Ireland and if they were landowners their estates became William's property.

The Civil Articles

The first Civil Article settled how much toleration Catholics would have from the new king.

A The first Civil Article

" . . . the Roman Catholics of this kingdom shall enjoy such privileges in the exercise of their religion, as are consistent with the laws of Ireland, or as they did enjoy in the reign of King Charles II."

Sarsfield and the Irish officers took the first article to mean freedom for Catholics to worship openly, and that they would have the same rights by law as Protestants. Ginkel knew that Catholics in Holland had complete freedom, so he had no doubt that William would allow Catholics in Ireland the same.

The rest of the treaty dealt with the status and rights of Jacobite landowners. It did not apply to officers who had been taken prisoner before the treaty nor to Catholic gentry living in places already occupied by Williamite forces. It only applied to civilians in Limerick and in other western areas which were still under Jacobite control and to Jacobite officers in those areas. They had to take an oath of loyalty to William. If they did this, they could keep their estates, enter the legal and medical professions and have the right, as gentlemen, to keep horses and arms for their own protection.

4 *In which ways might Catholics be disappointed by the Civil Articles?*

A broken treaty?

The terms about land ownership were quite clear and almost all the Catholic gentry who claimed they were entitled to keep estates were allowed to do so as soon as they had sworn loyalty to William.

The article which seemed to guarantee toleration for the Catholic Church was very vague. For one thing, in the reign of Charles II there had been laws against Catholics, but Charles himself and his officials in Ireland had simply not enforced them. So the words 'such privileges as they did enjoy in the reign of King Charles II' could mean different things to different families. Protestants could argue that Charles II had no right to be allowed such privileges.

The other phrase 'such privileges as are consistent with the laws of Ireland' was also a very unreliable guarantee. The laws were made by the Irish Parliament but the English Parliament claimed that its decisions could over-ride those made in Dublin. In 1691 it passed an Act which stated that no Catholics could sit in the Irish Parliament.

B Two Penal Laws

5 *What was the aim of each of these Acts?*

6 *How would Catholics argue that they did not break the treaty?*

7 *Explain how Protestants might argue that they did not break the treaty.*

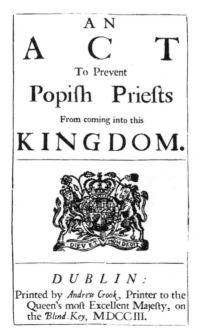

Parliament then passed a series of laws to weaken the social position of Catholics. They were known as the Penal Laws, from the way they penalised Catholics who held to their faith. In 1697 one of these Acts banished Catholic bishops and priests from the country. A few years later Parliament tried to stop the 'further growth of Popery' with a law which cut Catholics' rights to inherit or buy property – which meant that many would be too poor to qualify to hold public office. Another Penal Law forbade Catholics to open schools. Their general aim was to bring the whole Catholic population down to a level of poverty, ignorance and helplessness.

Catholics at home and those abroad in the armies of Louis XIV and later French kings had no doubt that the treaty had been broken. At the Battle of Fontenoy in 1745 between the French and the English the battle-cry from the ranks of the Irish Brigade recalled the events after Limerick.

C Battle-cry of the Irish Brigade, 1745

Cuimhnigí ar Luimneach
Remember Limerick

agus feall na Sasanach
and the treachery of the English

Who was to blame?

William signed the treaty in February 1692 and showed fairness to individual Catholic landowners, but he could not spend much time overseeing affairs in Ireland. He let the Protestant gentry keep Ireland quiet because he had to govern and defend England and Holland, keep on good terms with his allies and co-operate with the Dutch, English, Scottish and Irish parliaments.

The Irish Parliament, representing the Protestant gentry, had not been consulted about the terms of the treaty. Protestants generally thought the treaty far too lenient towards the people who had supported James. The Jacobite army had been allowed to go to France, with the main purpose of helping to defeat William and to restore James II to the throne of Ireland, and perhaps of England as well. Nothing in the treaty bound them not to do this. The Protestants were afraid that James would return with French and Irish troops who would be joined by their fellow-Catholics. Most Protestants were determined to prevent this if they possibly could.

1 *Suppose there had been a supreme authority like an International Court. What evidence would it have considered in deciding whether or not the Treaty of Limerick had been broken?*

2 *In which ways was the Treaty of Limerick badly worded?*

3 *Who drew up the terms of the treaty and who were the rulers who later had the power to apply those terms? How does this help to explain whether or not the treaty was broken?*

16 After Limerick: How did land ownership change?

In 1688 Catholic nobles and gentry owned almost a quarter (22 per cent) of the land. By 1703 when the question about land-ownership was finally settled, Catholics owned only fourteen per cent of the land. How did this change come about and who were the new landowners?

Losers and gainers

Most of the landowners who had fought for James II were treated as rebels and their estates were confiscated by William. Those who were protected by the Treaty of Limerick were allowed to keep their land only if they stayed in Ireland and swore an oath of loyalty to William. All those who went to France lost their land. Altogether about a million acres were confiscated.

A special court was set up in Dublin to deal with each case. About 65 landowners were allowed to keep their land because William felt that he could trust them. The confiscated land was given as a reward to men who had helped to defeat the Jacobites. William gave Ginkel a large estate and the title of Earl of Athlone. A French Huguenot officer, Ruvigny, was also rewarded with land and the title of Earl of Galway. Two of William's Dutch advisers, Arnold van Keppel and William Bentinck, received the largest amounts of land.

The English Parliament was very displeased about this favouritism towards foreigners and passed the Resumption Act in 1700. William had to agree to it, much against his will. This Act confirmed only seven of William's grants of land and ordered all the rest to be sold. The money raised in this way helped to pay the cost of bringing Ireland under English rule. No Irish Catholics were allowed to buy any of this land.

A Land ownership 1688 and 1703

Key to maps

—— Bold lines denote boundary between the four provinces. Names of counties are shown by initial.

All, or nearly all owned by Protestants
Protestant 90%–100% Catholic 0%–10%

At least three-quarters owned by Protestants
Protestant 75%–90% Catholic 10%–25%

Half to three-quarters owned by Protestants
Protestant 50%–75% Catholic 25%–50%

Over half owned by Catholics
Protestant 0%–50% Catholic 50%–100%

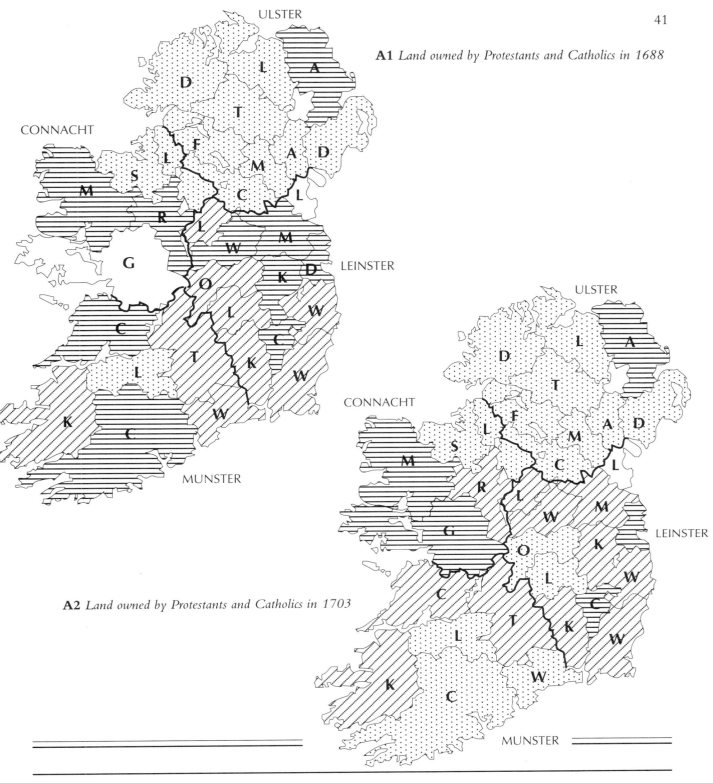

A1 *Land owned by Protestants and Catholics in 1688*

A2 *Land owned by Protestants and Catholics in 1703*

1. *Which province contained most Protestant-owned land in 1688?*

2. *Which province contained most Catholic-owned land in 1688?*

3. *In which province was there least change by 1703? Why was this?*

4. *In which two counties did most change take place?*

5. *In which five counties did Catholics own up to half the land in 1703?*

6. *In which two counties had Protestant landowning most sharply increased by 1703?*

7. *What percentage of land was owned by Catholics in your county in 1688? Did this change as a result of the Settlement? If so, how much did it change?*

17 After Limerick: Who were the Wild Geese?

Irish soldiers who went to France were known as the 'Wild Geese'. The geese that left Ireland each spring to fly north to their breeding grounds always returned in the autumn, and many people believed that the Wild Geese would also return.

How did the Irish Brigade start?

When the Jacobites lost control of Ulster in 1689 it was clear that they would need more experienced and better-equipped troops if they were to resist William's Dutch and German veterans. Louis XIV offered to send 6,000 French soldiers in exchange for about the same number of men from James II's Irish army. Louis was facing the combined forces of England, Holland, Spain, Austria and other German states, and he could not afford to send troops without replacements. The French contingent arrived at the end of March 1690 and five of the best Irish regiments were shipped to France. When they got to France, James's soldiers were reorganised into three regiments to form the Irish Brigade. They were given 'strangers' pay' which was slightly higher than the pay of ordinary French soldiers.

In October 1691, after the Treaty of Limerick, about 14,000 officers and men chose to go to France. They made the Irish Brigade up to twelve regiments. With new weapons and regular training they formed a valuable addition to the French army. Louis granted them French citizenship and they accepted the same pay as French soldiers.

In 1691 the Irish Parliament made it illegal for foreigners to recruit Irish soldiers. However, both France and Spain (who became an ally of France in 1700) continued to recruit soldiers in Ireland. In 1726 an agent of the Spanish king, Captain O'Nolan, was hanged for recruiting.

A Soldiers of the Irish Brigade in action, 1750

1   If you did not know who these men were, which European country might you think they came from?

2   What language(s) do you think these men spoke in 1750?

3   In what ways was the Irish Brigade at first different from the rest of the French army? How did its status change in 1691?

4   What does B tell you about foreign recruitment in the early eighteenth century?

B Captain O'Nolan's crime

"[He was condemned for having] . . . shipp'd off 200 men those two months past for the said service, and had a hundred more to go off that night . . ."

A chance to return?

It was only in Ireland that fighting ended in 1691. The war in Europe was still going on and no one knew whether England and her allies would defeat France. Many Irish people hoped that France would win and that James II, or later, his son, would be put back on the throne. Loyal Jacobites would then be given back their lands and Catholics would again be able to take part in the government.

The first French strike against William came in 1692, only a year after the Treaty of Limerick. Louis expected that William would transfer most of his troops to the European battlefronts. He therefore planned an invasion of England, which might succeed in restoring James to the throne, and would at least prevent William from sending more troops to the continent. The French invasion force consisted of 30,000 troops, about half of them men of the Irish Brigade, led by Sarsfield. They were ready to sail from Normandy in May 1692, but the French navy was defeated by the English and Dutch fleets. The Irish Brigade was sent to fight alongside other French regiments in the Netherlands, Germany, Italy and Spain.

The end of the Irish Brigade

England and France fought each other for long periods during the eighteenth century. Several other attempts were made to put James II's son on the throne but they were all defeated, some by storms and some by English sea-power.

C English fears of the Irish Brigade

5   *How might Irish officers expect to benefit from being loyal to James II?*

"As long as there is a body of Irish Roman Catholic troops abroad, the Chevalier [James II's son] will always make some figure in Europe . . . the hopes of being restored to their estates make the Irish officers daily wish for an occasion of exercising their aversion to [showing their dislike of] the present establishment."

(English pamphlet, 1727)

From about the middle of the eighteenth century France gave up any hope of restoring the Stuart monarchy in England. Illegal recruitment in Ireland came to an end and the Irish Brigade gradually became smaller. The sons and grandsons of pre-Williamite Catholic landowners continued to serve in the French and other armies. Some of them obtained high rank and titles of nobility as citizens of France, Spain and Austria. The Irish Brigade itself was finally disbanded during the French Revolution of 1789.

1   *Men who fight in another country's arms for pay are known as 'mercenaries'. What is the usual attitude to mercenaries in our own time? Does it make any more sense than the seventeenth-century view of them?*

2   *If the French invasion of England had taken place in 1692 what might have happened in Ireland?*

18 After Limerick: The fate of Catholic landowners

After the Treaty of Limerick many Catholic landowners went to France. What happened to those who stayed in Ireland?

Who were the rapparees?

Catholics who had laid down their arms before the treaty were classed as rebels and their land became William's property. Many of the smaller landowners among these 'rebels' became rapparees. They were like the victims of earlier land confiscations, the Tories, who had survived on help from their former tenants and by robbery.

Some rapparees believed that they were continuing the fight on behalf of King James, and at first only robbed people who supported William, particularly Protestant landowners. As time went on, however, they plundered and stole food, money and valuables wherever they could, and they became a danger to farmers, merchants and gentry – both Protestant and Catholic. They were hunted down by government troops and by the militia – part-time soldiers under the command of local Protestant magistrates.

A proclamation in the *Dublin Gazette* in February 1714 named about forty rapparees who were 'in arms and out upon their keeping'.

A A Proclamation, 1714

1 *What do you think is meant by 'in arms and out upon their keeping'?*

2 *Do you think the reward was enough to attract people?*

3 *Would the proclamation discourage people from helping the rapparees?*

"... if any Person or Persons whatsoever ... shall Kill, Apprehend or bring in the said Tories, Robbers or Rapparees ... every such Person ... shall receive from us the Sum of Twenty Pounds for each of the said Robbers.
    And We further Publish and Declare [that anyone] who shall knowingly Conceal, Aid, Abett or Succour [the rapparees] ... is Guilty of Felony ... and that we will have them Prosecuted accordingly with the utmost rigour."

A kind of pardon: the case of Donough MacCarthy

Some of the more important landowners tried to obtain a pardon from William. One was Donough MacCarthy, the only son of the Earl of Clancarty. He inherited an estate in Munster worth £9,000 a year when his father died in 1676. He married Lady Elizabeth Spencer, the daughter of the English Earl of Sunderland. MacCarthy became a junior officer in James II's Irish army and was taken prisoner when Cork surrendered in October 1690. He was put in the Tower of London and managed to escape to France but did not join the Irish Brigade. England and France made a temporary peace in 1697 and in 1698 Donough went back to England to see his wife. He was arrested again but this time he was pardoned by William. However, he was not given back his estates. Instead William gave him an allowance of £300 a year on condition that he never returned to England or Ireland. He and his wife went to live in Germany.

4 *Why would Donough MacCarthy not have been satisfied with £300 a year?*

5 *What suggests that he was not actively disloyal to William?*

The treatment of the loyal Catholic gentry

McCarthy's mother and three sisters petitioned William and the English Parliament for money to be paid to them from the family estates, but without success. Donough's only son, Robert, made a career in the British navy and became a senior officer. In 1734 when Donough died, Robert tried to recover his father's land. Some English nobles supported his request but the Irish Parliament refused to agree. As a result he left the navy and went to France where he helped to plan the 1745 Jacobite rebellion in Scotland. He died in France in 1770.

The treaty left about 14 per cent or one-seventh of the land of Ireland in the hands of Catholic landowners. They promised to be loyal to William but most of their Protestant neighbours suspected that they were still Jacobites at heart who might rebel if Louis XIV sent an invasion force.

The Irish Parliament passed the Penal Laws to reduce what little power and influence the Catholic gentry still had. One law was designed to split up Catholic estates. Normally, when a landowner died all his land was passed on to his eldest son. The law ordered that a Catholic's land was to be divided equally among all his sons. But if one son became a Protestant the entire estate was to go to him. Other laws banned Catholics from buying land and from obtaining land previously owned by Protestants.

Catholic landowners were excluded from any share in governing the country. They could not be Members of Parliament or army officers, county sheriffs or magistrates, nor could they vote. The law even forbade them to carry a sword and pistol and ride good quality horses – the accepted marks of a gentleman.

Lord Abercorn, a member of the Viceroy's Council, believed that this law was wrong:

B Lord Abercorn's criticism of the new law

" . . . [the Catholic gentry] are not only very few, but either of such quality and estate as it would be a shame to see walk without swords and ride without pistols
. . . exposed to such dangers from rogues."

6 *How might a Protestant MP argue a) for and b) against the laws which lowered the status of Catholic gentry?*

In some places Catholic landowners got round the laws because no one reported them. However, the only certain way to keep their position in society and to prevent estates being split up was to change their religion. Many of the larger landowners became Protestant and within two or three generations the percentage of Catholic-owned land fell from 14 per cent to only five per cent.

Do you think the treatment they were given would make Catholic landowners less or more likely to support the Jacobite cause?

19 After Limerick: The fate of ordinary Catholics

The laws passed by the Irish Parliament between 1695 and 1727 which penalised Catholics are known as the Penal Laws. How did they affect ordinary Catholics and their Church?

How was the Catholic Church affected?

All bishops and clergy, except parish priests, were banished and could face death if they returned. Parish priests were allowed to remain on condition that they registered with the authorities and recognised William as king. About a thousand stayed on these terms. However, the Catholic priesthood was expected to die out because no priests from abroad were allowed into the country and there were no bishops to ordain new ones. In fact some bishops did remain in hiding and clergy slipped in and out on continental shipping to keep the Catholic Church in Ireland in contact with Rome.

A Catholic chapel at Arles, County Leix built in the eighteenth century

1 *What does this picture suggest about the Catholics in the area?*

Parish priests often had to hold services in the open but sometimes money could be raised to build a simple chapel. Protestant gentry sometimes helped because they valued the work of priests in encouraging their people to be hardworking, sober and law-abiding. Priests could also be useful go-betweens for the landlord and the local peasants. Some landowners believed it was in their interests to be well-respected by tenants. For example a Protestant landowner in Fermanagh who found his peasants with a priest saying Mass in the open one very wet day allowed them to use his cow-house instead.

2 *Why did the Protestants not try harder to put an end to Catholicism?*

How were the Catholic middle classes affected?

Laws about education made it very difficult for middle-class Catholics to keep their position in society. No Catholic schools were allowed and it was illegal to send Catholic children to schools abroad. The only university, Trinity College, did not allow Catholics to take degrees. Even if they could somehow get sufficient education Catholics could not become lawyers, although they might be doctors.

No laws stopped well-off Catholics becoming merchants or traders but Protestants usually kept them out of the more profitable companies and guilds. Catholic craftsmen were forbidden to have more than two apprentices, unless they were in linen-weaving, so they had little chance to expand their businesses.

3 *What were the pressures on middle-class Catholics to become Protestants?*

All these difficulties and prohibitions prevented many middle-class families from improving or even maintaining their position in the community. Some of them, like some of the Catholic gentry, decided that they would have to become Protestants. If they did, they often dropped the prefix 'O' or 'Mac' or changed their surnames in some other way to make their origins less obvious.

How were the peasants affected?

The Catholic peasants did not own land and had no money to educate their sons, but they resented the low status of their own Church. They especially grudged having to pay tithes to the local Protestant minister as well as rent to the landlord and taxes to the government.

Where a new Protestant landowner replaced a Catholic gentleman the relationship between landlord and tenant changed. It was more natural for country people to turn to their priests to advise and lead them instead of approaching a landlord who no longer shared their religion and language.

The few Gaelic poets who had lived on the generosity of the old Catholic gentry now had to exist on the charity of the peasants, whom they had despised in former times. They complained bitterly that the new landlords were low-born money-grubbers, who thought only of making the most profit. In particular, they accused the landowners of making quick profits by clearing woodland by sale.

B A poet's comment

4 *How would clearing woods affect peasants' lives?*

"Cad a dhénanfamúid feasta gan adhmad?
What shall we do for timber?

Tá deireadh na gcoillte ar lár."
The last of the woods is down.

Other poems and songs kept alive the hope that the old Catholic gentry would one day return, helped by the French or the Spanish. Most peasants, however, were hard-headed enough to realise that this was a dream. Their main concern was to make a living as best they could.

---

1 *Do you think the Catholic peasants suffered more or less from the Penal Laws than the gentry and middle classes?*

2 *How did Catholics show their strong attachment to their faith? Are there any non-religious reasons which help to explain this?*

20 After Limerick: How were Presbyterians treated?

The greatest number of Protestants in Ulster were Presbyterians of Scottish descent. They were among the first to reject James II and played a very important part in his defeat. There were many laws against the Presbyterian Church but these were not enforced during the Williamite wars. The Presbyterians hoped that they would have complete freedom when the fighting was over. What happened was not what they expected.

Why did the Church of Ireland try to suppress the Presbyterians?

The people who set out to limit religious freedom for the Presbyterians were the Church of Ireland bishops and clergy and the landowners who controlled Parliament in Dublin. The Church of Ireland, like the Church of England, was part of the structure of government. Clergy and landowners believed that if the Presbyterians were not kept down, their own supremacy would be in danger.

In the years after 1691 the Catholics were defeated and leaderless, while the Presbyterians were well-organised. Thousands more Scots came to live in Ulster after the war and they were demanding complete freedom of worship. There had been 86 Presbyterian ministers in Ireland in 1689. By 1702 there were over 130. William had established the Presbyterian religion as the state Church of Scotland when the Scottish Parliament accepted him as king. Church of Ireland bishops were afraid that the Ulster Presbyterians would try to win the same status for themselves.

A A bishop on Scots immigration

1 *What did the writer mean by 'the Established Church'?*
2 *How did the Presbyterians seem more of a threat than the Catholics?*

" . . . [because] many Thousand Families . . . settling in this nation within these Five years . . . there is great reason to fear that when their Power and Numbers are increased, they will employ their Utmost Strength and most Vigorous Endeavours to Overturn . . . the Established Church."

(From a pamphlet by Tobias Pullein, Bishop of Dromore, 1697)

How were the Presbyterians kept in check?

Religious toleration was introduced by law in England for Protestant Dissenters in 1689, but the Irish Parliament refused to pass a similar law. This meant that Presbyterian ministers were not legally recognised as clergy so that marriages which they conducted were not legal. Until 1704 there was no ban on Presbyterians being members of town councils and some were elected as MPs. In 1704 however, Parliament passed an Act which disallowed Presbyterians from any part in local or central government. They were in almost the same inferior position as the Catholics, and like them, they also had to pay tithes to the Church of Ireland.

Irish Protestant bishops and landlords calculated that however much the Presbyterians raged against the laws, they would always join in resisting any possible Jacobite invasion or rebellion. King William, however, did show some gratitude. He prevented judges from punishing Presbyterians for not attending their local parish churches, which they were still legally supposed to do. But he could not persuade his Irish Parliament to grant religious toleration, and his English Parliament never paid the wages of the citizen soldiers who had defended Londonderry in his name. Eventually in 1719, during the reign of George I, Presbyterians were allowed freedom of worship, but they still could not be town councillors or Members of Parliament.

How did the Presbyterians react?

Some Presbyterians, like some Catholics, took the hard decision to change their Church in order to safeguard themselves and their families. Many stuck to their beliefs, and left Ireland to live in Pennsylvania and other North American colonies, where there was religious freedom, and plenty of land for families who were prepared to make a new life for themselves. When the first colonists became established others followed in hundreds. By the 1770s it was estimated that 12,000 people were emigrating from Ulster every year.

This emigration began about 1717 when many a farmer found that his lease was coming to an end. When a new lease was offered, most landlords increased the rent. If the farmer could not pay he had to leave the farm. If he did not leave willingly he could be evicted. A letter from a landlord's agent in County Down describes a common incident.

B An eviction

3   *What is meant by 'distraining'? What would the agent have done if he had found any articles of value in the farmhouse?*

4   *How does the letter tell us that Jas. Kerby had stayed in the farm for some time without paying rent?*

"I got into Jas. Kerby's house and turned him out and put Patrick Fling into possession. I did not find anything worth distraining, there not being in my opinion goods value 5 shillings, little wooden cups and trenchers [plates] 4 or 5, and all the hopes I have to get any of the arrears from him is by arresting him."

C A Presbyterian emigrant's house

5   *How would this house and land compare with their farm in Ulster? What does your answer suggest about the reasons why so many Presbyterians emigrated?*

(A log house in North Carolina)

It is 1719 and you overhear a conversation between two Presbyterians who had been in Londonderry during the siege. How would they argue for and against the advantages of having helped to put William on the throne thirty years before?

21 After Limerick: Who ruled Ireland?

Up to the beginning of the seventeenth century the king of England was the only ruler of his people but wise kings paid attention to their parliaments. King and Parliament were expected to work together as partners – but there was no doubt that the king was the senior partner. In the mid-seventeenth century the English Civil War was fought, the monarchy was abolished and then restored by Parliament. Finally William of Orange was made king – again by Parliament, which was now the senior partner. As England ruled Ireland, how did this change affect Ireland?

The parliaments and the king

The main reason why William had to do as his English Parliament wished was because they controlled the money which he spent on his army, navy, judges and officials. In the same way, William found that he had to agree to what the Irish Parliament wanted to obtain money to govern Ireland. William wanted to carry out the terms of the Treaty of Limerick in a more sympathetic way and treat the Catholics more fairly, but he hesitated to go against the Irish Parliament. He also could not insist that Parliament should give religious freedom to Presbyterians.

1   *How were both parliaments able to overrule the king?*

As king of Ireland, William was also powerless against the English Parliament. In 1700 he had to agree to the Resumption Act which cancelled most of his grants of land in Ireland.

The English Parliament and the Irish Parliament

The English Parliament claimed the right to make laws which affected Ireland. It passed an Act in 1691 to prevent Catholics from being members of the Irish Parliament. This was also what most Protestant Irish landowners wanted so they did not object. Their attitude was different when the English Parliament passed the Wool Act in 1699.

This Act stopped the export of wool and woollen cloth from Ireland. It killed a growing trade from which Protestant landowners and merchants could make a good profit. They complained loudly and one MP, William Molyneux, published a pamphlet titled 'The case of Ireland's being bound by acts of parliament in England, stated'. Molyneux tried to prove that the English Parliament had no right to make laws for Ireland.

Molyneux's supporters and many other Protestants considered themselves to be Englishmen living in Ireland, with the same rights as Englishmen living in England. They believed that they should have to obey only laws made by the parliament which they elected – the Irish Parliament. They could not complain too much, however, because they knew that they would need the power of England to protect them if a French attack and a Catholic uprising ever happened.

2   *Why did the Irish Parliament object to the English Parliament making laws for Ireland?*

3   *Why did they not insist that the English Parliament should stop doing that?*

The Irish House of Commons suggested in 1703 that there should be a union of England and Ireland, with a single Parliament. This would have been similar to the Union of England and Scotland which took place in 1707. The English Parliament did not like this idea. In 1719 they passed a law known as 'the Sixth [Act] of George I', declaring that the English Parliament had the right to make laws for Ireland, and that the highest court in England could overrule judgments made in Irish courts.

51

Who ruled Ireland?

The king still ruled both England and Ireland in the sense that he chose his ministers and advisers and appointed judges, bishops, generals, admirals and other high officials. He could not, however, make laws or change laws himself, and he had to govern in such a way as to satisfy Parliament.

The English Parliament was supreme over both England and Ireland, but allowed the Irish Parliament to make laws for Ireland so long as they did not claim equality, or do anything which might harm England's trade.

Ordinary people, Catholic peasants, Presbyterian farmers and linen-workers, and Protestant farmers and merchants had little or no say in what laws were made nor how they were enforced, and they never imagined they ought to have any say. For those who were dissatisfied and daring enough to make a change there were possibilities abroad. Catholic young men might become Wild Geese. Presbyterians might emigrate to a freer life in America. But the stage was set for a century in which Protestant landowners, clergy and professional people would dominate social and political life in Ireland.

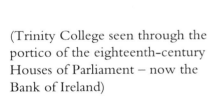

A Two symbols of the Protestant ascendancy

4 *Explain how Parliament and Trinity College symbolised the ascendancy.*

(Trinity College seen through the portico of the eighteenth-century Houses of Parliament – now the Bank of Ireland)

1 *Look back at the question at the end of Unit 1. What do you now think about these questions?*
   a) *Are Catholics and Nationalists correct in thinking of the Treaty of Limerick as a broken treaty? If so, who was most responsible for breaking it?*
   b) *Did Ulster Presbyterians have any grounds for hero-worshipping William of Orange?*
   c) *Would Church of Ireland Protestants have reasons for being completely satisfied with the result of the War of the Two Kings?*
   d) *How much had the War of the Two Kings to do with the Irish affairs?*

2 *How would you now answer the questions:*
   Why remember the Boyne?
   Why remember the Treaty of Limerick?